M. B. EMENEAU

SANSKRIT SANDHI AND EXERCISES

REVISED EDITION

Berkeley and Los Angeles 1966
UNIVERSITY OF CALIFORNIA PRESS

University of California Press

Berkeley and Los Angeles

California

Cambridge University Press

London, England

Fifth Printing, 1966

To

The Memory of

LEONARD BLOOMFIELD

(1887-1949)

INTRODUCTORY NOTE

Sanskrit has long been taught in conjunction with the elements of Indo-European historical grammar. Its potentialities as a means of induction of students into methods of descriptive grammar have seldom been utilized in an explicit way. And this in spite of the honored priority and eminence of Pāṇini (? circa 5th century B.C.) as a descriptive grammarian and of William Dwight Whitney (1827–1894) as an arranger of Pāṇini's grammar for Western use. Perhaps the chief reason for this neglect is the fact that Whitney's Sanskrit Grammar is not in form a perfect beginner's book, even though his famous use of large and small print was intended to make it that. The device breaks down in chapter III, "Rules of euphonic combination," where much that even the beginner needs to know is given in small print and it is therefore impossible for the beginner in Sanskrit or for the non-Sanskritist descriptivist to find his way around with any ease. Nor do any of the professed beginner's books really make good this deficiency.

On occasion Leonard Bloomfield, to whose memory this pamphlet is dedicated, taught beginning Sanskrit in the Linguistic Institute. In the Institute of 1938 he handed over to me a class that he had begun and the notes that he had prepared for his own use. These included the selection of sandhi rules from Whitney's chapter III that he thought it necessary for a beginner to have an acquaintance with. Since that time I have, with his permission given initially, used and reworked these notes. They have been found so useful by myself and successive classes of students that it seems worthwhile to present them in printed form, along with a set of 27 exercises that I have constructed to give the student that familiarity with the rules that will fix them firmly with him. It is thought too that even a student of descriptive grammar could be given these exercises to work, without his knowing or learning any more Sanskrit than is provided in the pamphlet. The exercises do not proceed in the usual direction of those set e.g. by Nida, but to reconstruct from Pāṇini's solutions the complicated data from which he started should give students practice in handling complicated data with exactness (which many of them fail in) and a feeling for the techniques of morphological analysis.

The particular style of statement used by Pāṇini, Whitney, and many other grammarians is one that is slightly out of fashion now. Yet it is a productive style and students in descriptive grammar should be taught to operate with it. Pāṇini set up for every polyallomorphic morpheme one of the allomorphs as a basic form (e.g., the verb root or the noun stem as basic to all forms of a complex verb or noun paradigm), and established a very complicated set of morphophonemic statements to describe the relations between the basic allomorphs and all allomorphs related to them. These morphophonemic statements are the sandhi rules of Whitney's chapter III and are stated in terms of process. Such statement is harmless if the student understands that it is descriptive process that is involved, and not historical. Consequently, Whitney's phraseology is not departed from very much in the sandhi rules here given; references are always given to Whitney (e.g. W241) and a violent departure from his words would have defeated the object of framing the essential set of rules.

The older readers of the pamphlet will recognize at once the influence of Bloomfield in the more Paninean and less Whitney-like overall arrangement and phrasing of the sandhi rules. Bloomfield was indeed an admirer of Pāṇini (others can vouch for this better than I), and all my changes of phrasing have not concealed this. But, thanks in large part to Bloomfield, we now all tend to approximate Pāṇini rather than Whitney in the style of our descriptive statements. In one major point Whitney has been left and Pāṇini's use of a morphophonemic symbol has been readopted, i.e. the use of ṝ in a number of verb roots (rule 39; W242a). Whitney's phonetic terms are now old-fashioned; the equations between his and mine will be self-evident. One transcriptional symbol differs from that used by Whitney; ś is now generally used in this country and elsewhere instead of ç for the palatal sibilant.

BIBLIOGRAPHY

William Dwight Whitney, Sanskrit Grammar, (2d ed.; Cambridge, Mass., Harvard University Press, 1889), with many re-issues.

THE PHONEMES (W5)

Vowels	velar	palatal	labial	retroflex	dental
simple					
short	a	i	u	ṛ	ḷ
long	ā	ī	ū	ṝ	
diphthongal					
short		e	o		
long		āi	āu		

Visarga ḥ

Anusvāra ṃ

Consonants	velar	palatal	retroflex	dental	labial
Mutes					
unvoiced plain stops	k	c	ṭ	t	p
unvoiced aspirated stops	kh	ch	ṭh	th	ph
voiced plain stops	g	j	ḍ	d	b
voiced aspirated stops	gh	jh	ḍh	dh	bh
voiced nasals	n̄	ñ	ṇ	n	m
Semivowels					
voiced		y	r	l	v
Sibilants					
unvoiced		ś	ṣ	s	
Aspirate					
voiced h					

Phonemes occurring at the ends of words in absolutely final position in sentence (W122):

vowel   visarga   k n̄ ṭ ṇ t n p m   l

GUṆA AND VṚDDHI SUBSTITUTIONS

Substitutes in morphology for vowels (W235-236):

basic vowels	a	i, ī	u, ū	ṛ, ṝ	ḷ
guṇa	a	e	o	ar	al
vṛddhi	ā	āi	āu	ār	āl

A few verbs have reverse guṇa and vṛddhi, but instead of their roots being stated with the basic vowels, they are stated with reverse guṇa (e.g., vac- instead of uc-, yaj- instead of ij-, prach- instead of pṛch-) (W241, 252).

basic vowels	i	u	ṛ
guṇa	ya	va	ra
vṛddhi	yā	vā	rā

SANDHI

The rules that follow do not give all the sandhi statements that are made by Pāṇini and Whitney. However, in general, all other occurring combinations of phonemes than those dealt with in the rules remain unchanged, except for special statements that are given in the morphology rather than in the sandhi rules.

EXTERNAL SANDHI

Operates between words in phrases, and between members of a compound (W109b).

Operates also at the ends of noun stems before the case endings beginning with bh and s (W111a), and often before secondary derivative suffixes beginning with consonants other than y (W111d); within the words so formed, however, the internal sandhi rules affecting s and n (rules 46 and 47) operate in the suffixes.

Vowels

1. Like simple vowels coalesce to the corresponding long vowel (W126). E.g. tatra 'there' + asti 'he, she, it is' > tatrā 'sti; tathā 'thus' + asti > tathā 'sti 'thus it is'; tatra + āste 'he, she sits' > tatrā 'ste 'there he (or she) sits'; ati 'exceedingly' + iva 'as it were' > atī 'va 'exceedingly.'

2. a or ā plus an unlike simple vowel, yields guṇa of the second vowel (W127). E.g. tatra 'there' + icchati 'he desires' > tatre 'cchati; tathā 'thus' + icchati > tathe 'cchati; tathā + uktam 'it is said' > tatho 'ktam; brahma- 'priest' + ṛṣi- 'sage' > brahmarṣi- 'a sage who is a priest.'

3. a or ā plus a diphthong, yields the corresponding long diphthong (W127). E.g. tatra 'there' + eti 'he, she, it goes' > tatrāi 'ti.

4. Other simple vowels before unlike vowels are replaced by the corresponding semivowels (W129). E.g. asti 'there is' + asmin deśe 'in this country' > asty asmin deśe; iti 'thus' (after directly quoted speech) + uktvā 'having said' > ity uktvā 'having said this.'

5. After a short diphthong initial a is elided (W135). E.g. vane 'in the forest' + asti 'he, she, it is' > vane 'sti.

6. e before any other vowel than a is replaced by a, and hiatus remains (W133). E.g. vane 'in the forest' + iha 'here' > vana iha 'in this forest.'

7. āi before a vowel is replaced by ā, and hiatus remains (W133). E.g. tasmāi 'to him' + adadāt 'he gave' > tasmā adadāt.

8. o before any other vowel than a, and āu before all vowels, are replaced by av and āv respectively (W134b). E.g. tāu 'the two of them' + atra 'here' > tāv atra.

9. After a short vowel, the preposition ā, and the adverb mā, ch is written cch; after other long vowels, optionally. I.e. ch is phonemically always equal to two consonants and is written so where it might be ambiguous for metrical purposes and in several other places. (W227) E.g. tava 'your' + chāyā 'shadow' > tava cchāyā.

10. There is no sandhi after the dual endings ī, ū, and e, or after the nominative plural masculine pronoun form amī, or after an interjection consisting of one vowel (e.g. a), or

after o ending a particle (e.g. aho); this is called pragṛhya (W138). E.g. yajete 'the two of them sacrifice' + ubhāu 'both men' > yajete ubhāu 'both of them sacrifice.'

<u>s</u> <u>and</u> <u>r</u> <u>in</u> <u>final</u> <u>position</u> <u>in</u> <u>the</u> <u>word</u>

11. -s and -r, final in phrase or before a sibilant or a voiceless labial or velar stop, are replaced by ḥ (W170a, 170d, 172, 178a). E.g. manus 'Manu'+ svayam 'himself' > manuḥ svayam 'Manu himself'; yaśas 'fame' + prāpa 'he obtained' > yaśaḥ prāpa 'he obtained fame'; puruṣas 'man' + khanati 'he digs' > puruṣaḥ khanati 'the man is digging'; punar 'again' + khanati > punaḥ khanati 'he is digging again.'

12. -s and -r, before a voiceless palatal, retroflex, or dental stop, are replaced by the sibilant corresponding to the stop (W170c, 178a). E.g. tatas 'then' + ca 'and' > tataś ca 'and then'; cakṣus 'eye' + te 'your' > cakṣus te 'your eye.'

13. -as plus initial a yield o (W175a). E.g. devas 'god' + asti 'there is' > devo 'sti 'there is a god.'

14. -as before any other vowel than a loses s and hiatus remains (W175c). E.g. devas + āste 'he sits' > deva āste 'the god is sitting'; devas + iha 'here' > deva iha.

15. -as before a voiced consonant is replaced by o (W175a). E.g. devas + gacchati 'he goes' > devo gacchati 'the god is going'; devas + rocate 'he shines' > devo rocate 'the god shines.'

16. -ās before a voiced sound loses s, and if the voiced sound is a vowel, hiatus remains (W177). E.g. devās 'gods' + gacchanti 'they go' > devā gacchanti 'the gods are going'; devās + āsate 'they sit' > devā āsate 'the gods are sitting.'

17. Any other case of -s and any case of -r, before r is dropped with lengthening of the preceding vowel if it is short (there is no instance of ṙr in the language) (W179). E.g. agnis 'fire' + rocate 'it shines' > agnī rocate 'the fire shines'; punar 'again' + rocate > punā rocate 'it shines again.'

18. Any other case of -s before any voiced sound other than r, is replaced by r (W174). E.g. agnis + asti > agnir asti 'there is a fire'; agnis 'the god of fire' + gacchati > agnir gacchati 'the god of fire is going.'

19. <u>But</u>, bhos 'O respected sir!' before voiced sounds drops s (W174b). E.g. bho bho deva 'Hail! hail! O god!'

20. sas 'he' and esas 'this man' drop s before any consonant

(W176a). E.g. sas + gacchati > sa gacchati 'he is going'; sas + brāhmaṇas 'a brahman' > sa brāhmaṇaḥ 'that brahman.'

21. Any other case of -r remains, i.e. before other voiced sounds than itself (W178). E.g. punar 'again' + gacchati > punar gacchati 'he is going again'; punar + asti 'he is' > punar asti.

Nasals

22. -m before a consonant is replaced by anusvāra (W213i). E.g. devam 'god (accusative case)' + paśyati 'he sees' > devaṃ paśyati 'he sees the god.'

23. -n before a voiceless palatal, retroflex, or dental stop is replaced by anusvāra plus the sibilant homorganic with the stop (W208). E.g. aśvān 'horses (accusative case)' + corayati 'he steals' > aśvāṃś corayati 'he steals horses'; bhavān 'the respected person' + tarkayatu 'let him reflect' > bhavāṃs tarkayatu 'let your honor reflect.'

24. -n before a voiced palatal or retroflex stop is replaced by the nasal homorganic with the stop (ñ, ṇ) (W202b, 205b). E.g. devān 'gods (accusative case)' + jayati 'he conquers' > devāñ jayati 'he conquers the gods.'

25. -n plus ś- are replaced by -ñ ch- (W203). E.g. devān + śṛṇoti 'he hears' > devāñ chṛṇoti 'he hears the gods.'

26. -n before l- is replaced by anusvāra plus l (W206). E.g. aśvān + labhate 'he receives' > aśvāṃl labhate 'he receives horses.'

27. The velar, retroflex, or dental nasal after a short vowel and before a vowel, is doubled (W210). E.g. hasan 'smiling' + agacchat 'he went' > hasann agacchat.

Stops

28. -t before a voiceless palatal or retroflex stop is replaced by the corresponding voiceless unaspirated stop (i.e. c or ṭ) (W202a, 199a). E.g. tat 'that' + ca 'and' > tac ca 'and that'; tat + ṭīkā- 'commentary' > taṭṭīkā- 'commentary on that.'

29. -t before a voiced palatal or retroflex stop is replaced by the corresponding voiced unaspirated stop (i.e. j or ḍ) (W202a, 199a). E.g. tat + jalam 'water' > taj jalam 'that water.

30. -t before l- is replaced by l (W162). E.g. tat + labhate 'he receives' > tal labhate 'he receives that.'

31. -t plus ś- are replaced by -c ch- (W203). E.g. tat + śṛṇoti 'he hears' > tac chṛṇoti 'he hears that.'

32. A stop before a nasal is replaced by the nasal in the position of the stop (W161). E.g. vāk 'voice' + mama 'my' > vāñ mama 'my voice'; tat + mitram 'friend' > tan mitram 'that friend.'

33. A stop plus h- are replaced by the voiced unaspirated stop plus the voiced aspirated stop, both homorganic with the original final stop (W163). E.g. tat + hiraṇyam 'gold' > tad dhiraṇyam 'that gold.'

34. In all other instances, a voiceless stop before a voiced sound is replaced by the corresponding (unaspirated) voiced stop (W157c, 159). E.g. vāk 'voice' + asti 'there is' > vāg asti 'there is a voice'; ap- 'water' + ja- 'born of' > abja- 'lotus (born of the water).' (The reverse rule, concerning assimilation of a voiced stop to a following voiceless sound, has little scope except in such forms as bhiṣaj- 'physician' [> bhiṣag- (rule 61)] + -su 'locative plural' > bhiṣakṣu 'among the physicians.' Words are put into sentences and stems into compounds, starting from their basic forms, i.e. from the forms they have in absolutely final position [except for those ending in -s and -r]; consequently, no voiced stops occur at their ends [see statement on phonemes].)

INTERNAL SANDHI

Operates in all cases of the junction of morphemes except those covered by the external sandhi statements.

Vowels

35-37. Identical with rules 1-3. E.g. a-as-ī-t > āsīt 'he, she, it was'; bhava-ī-t > bhavet 'he, she, it would be'; deva-āu > devāu 'two gods.'

38. Final short or long i and u of a monosyllabic root, before a vowel are replaced by iy and uv respectively (W129a). E.g. strī- 'woman' + -am 'accusative singular' > striyam; bhū- 'earth' + -am > bhuvam. <u>But</u>, y-anti 'they go' and y-antu 'let them go' from the verb root i- 'go' (Pāṇini 6.4.81). In the weak forms of the perfect (i.e. all except the singular active), verbs ending in u and ū follow this rule (except bhū- 'become, be'); verbs in ī follow the general rule (rule 40).

39. Final ṝ of a root (whether verb or noun), after a labial consonant and before a vowel, is replaced by ur; not before a vowel, by ūr. After other consonants than labials and before a vowel, it is replaced by ir; not before a vowel, by īr (W242). E.g. pṝ- 'city' + -am 'accusative singular' > puram; pṝ- + -s

or zero 'nominative singular' > pūr (> pūḥ [rule 11]); kṝ- 'scatter' : kirati 'he scatters,' kīryate 'it is scattered.' This rule works in the description of many forms; others show the regular morphological replacement by guṇa and vṛddhi. In noun forms the replacement by īr and ūr takes place first in the description, and then the internal sandhi rules operate before case endings beginning with a consonant.

40. Short ṛ and other cases of short or long i and u than those covered in rule 38, before a vowel are replaced by the corresponding semivowels (W129). E.g. pitṛ- 'father' + -os 'genitive or locative dual' > pitros; juhu- 'sacrifice (present stem)' + -ati > juhvati 'they sacrifice.'

41. A diphthong before a vowel is replaced by short or long a (depending on whether it is a short or long diphthong) plus the corresponding semivowel (W131). E.g. agne- (stem with guṇa of final vowel of agni- 'fire') + -e 'dative singular' > agnaye 'to the fire.'

Consonants

42. All but the first consonant of a cluster drops at the end of a word (W150b). E.g. bharant- 'carrying' + -s or zero 'nominative singular masculine' > bharan 'he who carries.'

43. But, r plus a stop is kept, if the stop belongs to the stem (W150b). E.g. suhārd- 'friend' + -s or zero > suhārt (cf. rule 57).

44. A dental stop or nasal after a retroflex consonant (but not after r) is replaced by the corresponding retroflex (W197, 198). E.g. dviṣ- 'hate' + -ta- 'perfect passive participle' > dviṣṭa- 'hated'; ji- 'win' + -snu- (makes adjectives from verb roots) > jiṣṇu- 'victorious' (s > ṣ according to rule 46, then n > ṇ according to this rule).

45. ch after a vowel is replaced by cch (W227). E.g. agacchat 'he went' (root gam- 'go' has allomorph gach- in the present and imperfect).

46. s after a vowel other than short or long a, or after k, r, or l, is replaced by ṣ, unless final or followed by r; anusvāra or visarga intervening between a vowel and s does not prevent the replacement, except in puṃs- 'man,' hiṃs- 'injure,' and a few other words (W180). E.g. agni- 'fire' + -su 'locative plural' > agniṣu 'among the fires'; vāk- (vāc- 'word' with c > k according to rule 59) + -su > vākṣu 'among the words.' But, there are a few exceptions to the rule, e.g. kusuma- 'flower.'

47. n, when preceded anywhere in the same word by r, ṣ, ṛ or ṝ with no intervening palatal, retroflex, or dental consonant (except y), and at the same time followed immediately by a vowel, semivowel, or nasal, is replaced by ṇ (W189). E.g. nara- 'man': narāṇām 'of the men'; brahman- 'priest; prayer': brahmaṇya- 'pious.' There are a few words in which ṇ occurs without the operation of this rule, e.g. puṇya- 'meritorious,' guṇa- 'quality.'

48. A nasal before a stop is replaced by the nasal homorganic with the stop (W212). E.g. the nasal infix -n- is assimilated in yuñjmas 'we join,' yuṅgdhi 'join!'

49. A nasal before a sibilant is replaced by anusvāra (W204). E.g. man- 'think': maṃsyate 'he will think.'

50. m before v and m is replaced by n (W212a). E.g. gam- 'go': aganva 'we two went,' aganma 'we (plural) went.'

51. n after a palatal stop (c, j) is replaced by the palatal nasal (ñ) (W201). E.g. yaj- 'sacrifice' + -na- > yajña- 'a sacrifice.'

52. s between stops disappears (W233c-f). E.g. chid- 'cut': acchitta 'he cut' (< a-chid-s-ta; cf. rule 57). This rule can also be invoked to explain pumbhis 'by the men' < pums- + -bhis (W394).

53. h in the root han 'strike, slay' is replaced by gh when the vowel of the root disappears (W2161). E.g. han-mi 'I kill: ghn-anti 'they kill.'

54. In certain roots, whenever final h or a voiced aspirated stop is replaced by an unaspirated stop, the initial of the root (being a voiced unaspirated stop) becomes aspirated, unless by the rules following this one the final consonant of the root plus a consonant of the suffix result in a cluster ending in a voiced aspirated stop (W155).

Roots:

dah- 'burn (transitive)'
dih- 'smear'
duh- 'milk'
druh- 'hurt'
dṛṃh- 'make firm'
guh- 'conceal, hide'
bandh- 'bind'
bādh- 'harass, resist'
budh- 'be awake'

and a few other roots in one or two forms only (note especially dh as initial reduplicating consonant in various forms of the verb dhā- 'place' [see rules 55-57]). E.g. dogdhi 'he milks': adhok 'he milked.'

But, certain forms occur with two aspirates: 2d plural verb forms in the middle voice, present indicative, imperfect indicative, present imperative; e.g. from the root duh-: dhugdhve, adhugdhvam, dhugdhvam. Also instrumental plurals of nouns; e.g. from root budh-, -bhudbhis 'by those who are awakened to . . . .'

55. Voiced aspirated stop plus t or th yield voiced unaspirated stop plus dh (W160). E.g. budh- 'be awakened' + -ta- 'perfect passive participle' > buddha- 'who is awakened'; labh- 'receive' + -ta- > labdha- 'which has been received.' But, the following more general rules apply to the present-tense forms of dhā- 'place' made from the reduplicated weak form dadh- (W667-668) and to its desiderative.

56. Aspirated stop before a stop, a sibilant, or zero yields the corresponding unaspirated stop (W141, 153). E.g. likh- 'paint': citralik 'a painter of pictures.'

57. Voiced stop before an unvoiced consonant or zero is replaced by the corresponding unvoiced stop (W141, 159). E.g. vid- 'know': vetsi 'you know'; budh- 'be awakened': bhotsyate 'he will be awakened.'

58. Unvoiced stop before voiced stop is replaced by the corresponding voiced stop (W159). E.g. śak- 'help': śagdhi 'help!'

When final in word, or when followed by any other sound than a vowel, semivowel, or nasal (the following statements 59 to 71 apply):

59. c is treated as k (W217). E.g. vac- 'say': vakṣyati 'he will say,' vagdhi 'say!', ukta- 'which has been said.'

60. j is normally treated as g (W219a). E.g. yuj- 'join': yokṣyati 'he will join,' yuṅgdhi 'join!', yukta- 'which has been joined.' (The reason for treatment as g rather than k is the perfect passive participles in Exercise 15, nos. 12 and 13.)

61. h in roots with initial d, in noun uṣṇih- (name of a meter), and optionally in roots druh- 'hurt,' snih- 'be moist,' and muh- 'be bewildered,' is treated as gh (W222a). E.g. duh- 'milk': dhokṣyati 'he will milk,' dugdhi 'milk!', dugdha- 'which has been milked.'

62. jh is treated as k (W220b; a grammarian's statement, with no occurrences!).

63. kṣ in jakṣ- 'eat' is treated as gh (W221a, 233f). E.g jagdha- 'which has been eaten.'

64. In the roots bhṛj- 'fry, roast,' bhrāj- 'shine,' mṛj- 'wipe,' yaj- 'sacrifice,' rāj- 'rule,' sṛj- 'send away, emit; twine,' and in the noun parivrāj- 'wandering mendicant' (but not in the nouns ṛtvij- 'priest' from yaj-, and sraj- 'wreath' from sṛj-):

j final is replaced by ṭ,
j before s is replaced by k in verb forms, by ṭ in noun forms,
j before bh (in noun forms), is replaced by ḍ,
j before dh, is replaced by ḍ,
j before t, is replaced by ṣ (W219b-c).

E.g. yakṣyati 'he (the priest) will sacrifice'; mṛḍḍhi 'rub!'; mṛṣṭvā 'having rubbed'; parivrāṭ 'religious mendicant (nominative singular).'

65. Similarly, ch (the only examples are from the root prach- 'ask'; W220). E.g. prakṣyati 'he will ask,' pṛṣṭvā 'having asked,' aprāṭ 'he asked.'

66. Similarly, śc (the only examples are from the root vraśc- 'cut down, hew'; W221b). E.g. vrakṣyati 'he will hew,' vṛṣṭvā 'having cut down.'

67. Similarly, ś (W218); <u>but</u>, in the roots diś- 'point, show,' dṛś- 'see,' mṛś- 'touch,' spṛś- 'touch,' and optionally in naś- 'be lost; attain,' ś when final and in noun forms before s and bh, is treated as k (W218a). E.g. viś- 'tribe': viṭ (nominative singular), viṭsu (locative plural), viḍbhis (instrumental plural); diś- 'show, point': dekṣyati 'he will show,' diṣṭa- 'which has been shown,' dik 'direction (nominative singular).'

68. Similarly (to j), kṣ normally (W221). E.g. takṣ- 'fashion as a carpenter': takṣyati 'he will fashion,' taṣṭa- 'fashioned.'

69. Similarly, ṣ normally (W226). E.g. dviṣ- 'be hostile, hate': dviṭ 'enemy (nominative singular),' dvekṣyati 'he will be hostile,' dviṣṭa- 'hated,' dviḍḍhi 'hate!'

70. h in nah- 'bind, tie' is treated as dh (W223g). E.g. natsyati 'he will tie,' naddha- 'tied.'

71. Normal treatment of h (W222b):

h plus t, th, dh are replaced by ḍh with lengthening of a preceding a, i, u; <u>but</u>, vah- 'carry' and sah- 'overcome' have o instead of lengthened a;

h before s, is replaced by k in verb forms, ṭ in noun forms,
h before bh (in noun forms), is replaced by ḍ,
h final, is replaced by ṭ.

E.g. lih- 'lick' : leḍhi 'he licks,' līḍha- 'licked,' lekṣyati 'he will lick,' madhuliṭ 'bee (nominative singular),' madhuliḍbhis 'by the bees.'

72. s before s is replaced by t in certain forms (W167). E.g. vas- 'dwell' : vatsyati 'he will dwell.'

73. s before dh is replaced by zero (W166). E.g. śās- 'chastise, rule, teach' : śādhi 'chastise!'

Exercise 1

A. Put the words together in sentences or phrases, in the order in which they are given.

1. atha (adverb 'now begins new subject') + ādiparva ('first book of the Mahābhārata [nominative singular]').
2. trīṇi ('three [neuter]') + indriyāṇi ('senses')
3. atha + udyogaparva ('fifth book of the Mahābhārata [nominative singular]').
4. ādiparva (see 1; accusative singular) + eva (adverb 'just what the previous word says and nothing else') + paṭhati ('he is reading').
5. āraṇyakaparvaṇi ('in the third book of the Mahābhārata') + eva + nalopākhyānam ('story of Nala' [nominative singular]') + asti ('is')

6, 7. asti ('there is, was') + asmin ('in that' with masculine or neuter noun in locative case) + pradeśe ('in a place') + aśvaḥ ('a horse [nominative]').

8. asti + asmin + pradeśe + ṛṣiḥ ('a sage [nominative]').
9. asāu ('he') + āha ('he said').
10. kanye ('two girls') + āgacchataḥ ('the two of them are coming').

B. Put the stems together in compounds, in the order in which they are given.

1. rāja- ('king') + ṛṣi- ('sage'). Meaning: 'royal sage.'
2. madhu- ('honey') + utsava- ('festival'). Meaning: 'festival of spring.'
3. jñāna- ('knowledge') + indriya- ('organ of sense'). Meaning: 'sense organ.'
4. nala- (Nala, a man) + upākhyāna- ('story'). Meaning: 'story about Nala.'
5. sītā- (Sītā, a woman) + ūrmilā- (Ūrmilā, a woman). Meaning: 'Sītā and Ūrmilā.'
6. pitṛ- ('father') + artham ('for the sake of'). Meaning: 'for father's sake.'
7. māndhātṛ- (Māndhātṛ, a man) + upākhyāna-. Meaning: 'story about Māndhātṛ.'
8. strī- ('woman') + agāra- ('apartment'). Meaning: 'the women's apartments (in a palace).'
9. bhrātṛ- ('brother') + ṛṣi-. Meaning: 'the sage, (my) brother.'

10. go- ('cow, bull') + aśva- ('horse'). Meaning: 'cattle and horses.'

Exercise 2

Put the words together in sentences or phrases, in the order in which they are given.

1, 2, 3. havis ('offering [accusative]') + prāpsyati ('he will obtain') + agnis ('fire, the god of fire [nominative]').
4, 5. kukkuras ('dog [nominative]') + punar ('again') + khanati ('is digging').
6. tatra ('there') + puruṣas ('man [nominative]') + sthāsyati ('he will stand').
7. puruṣas + ca ('and') + khanati.
8. nalas ('Nala [nominative]') + abravīt ('he said').
9. nalas + eti ('he goes').
10. nalas + bādhyate ('he is in trouble').
11, 12. rājaputrās ('princes [nominative]') + āhus ('they said').
13. śaśās ('hares [nominative]') + bibhyati ('they are afraid').
14. devās ('gods [nominative]') + rocante ('they are brilliant').
15. śiśus ('boy [nominative]') + roditi ('he is weeping').
16. śiśus + jalpati ('he is chattering').
17. paraśubhis ('with axes') + akṛntan ('they cut').
18, 19. sas ('that [nominative masculine]') + puruṣas.
20, 21, 22. muhur (repeat this word, in meaning 'repeatedly') + cakṣus ('eye [accusative]') + nyamiṣat ('he winked').

Exercise 3

Put the words together in sentences or phrases, in the order in which they are given.

1. aham ('I') + trīn ('three [accusative masculine]') + puruṣān ('men [accusative]') + paśyāmi ('I see').
2. kasmin cid ('in a certain') + vane ('in a forest').
3. bhavān ('you [polite]') + tatra ('there') + tiṣṭhatu ('stand [imperative]').
4, 5, 6. sas ('that [nominative masculine]') + rājā ('king [nominative]') + asmān ('us [accusative]') + jeṣyati ('he will conquer').
7. tasmin ('in that') + śayane ('in a bed').
8, 9. trīn + lokān ('the worlds [accusative]') + jayati ('he conquers').
10. tasmin + araṇye ('in a jungle').

11-15. atas ('therefore') + aham + bravīmi ('I say') + upāyam ('a means [accusative]') + cintayet ('he should think of') + prājñas ('a wise man [nominative]') + iti (adverb ending quotation which begins with upāyam and ends with prājñas).

16-21. tatas ('then') + savismayam ('with amazement') + sarvāis ('by all the men') + dṛṣṭas ('he was seen') + pṛṣṭas ('he was asked') + ca ('and,' following B in 'A and B') + bhos ('sir! ') + kim ('what? ') + idam ('that').

22-25. sā ('she') + abravīt ('she said'). katham ('how? ') + ca + etat ('that'). sas ('he') + abravīt ('he said').

Exercise 4

A. Put the stems together in compounds, in the order in which they are given.

1. tat- ('that one') + chāyā- ('shadow'). Meaning: 'his shadow.'
2. tat- + jñāna- ('knowledge'). Meaning: 'knowledge of that.'
3. tat- + ḍiṇḍima- ('drum'). Meaning: 'his drum.'
4. vidyut- ('lightning') + lekhā- ('streak'). Meaning: 'a streak of lightning.'
5. tat- + śabda- ('word'). Meaning: 'that word.'
6. vidyut- + mālā- ('wreath'). Meaning: 'a wreath of lightning.'
7. vāk- ('word, voice') + madhura- ('sweet'). Meaning: 'sweet of speech.'
8. vāk- + hasta- ('hand') + -vant- ('possessing'). Meaning: 'possessing speech and hands.'
9. tat- + gṛha- ('house'). Meaning: 'his house.'
10. vāk- + īśa- ('master, lord'). Meaning: 'author, poet.'

B. Put the words together in sentences, in the order in which they are given.

1, 2. kīlakas ('wedge [nominative]') + sthānāt ('from its place') + caliṣyati ('it will move').

3, 4, 5. yat ('what [relative nominative singular neuter]') + vṛttam ('happened') + tat ('that [demonstrative nominative singular neuter]') + bhavatā ('by you [polite]') + viditam ('it is known').

6-10. kadā cit ('once upon a time') + vānarayūthas ('a herd of monkeys') + itas ('this way') + tatas ('that way') + ca ('and,' following B in 'A and B') + krīḍan ('playing') + āgatas ('it came').

Exercise 5

A. From the following verb roots make the 3rd plural perfect by initial reduplication of the vowel of the root and adding the suffix -us.

1. as- 'be.' 2. āp- 'obtain.' 3. i- 'go' (apply rule 38, then reduplication). 4. iṣ- 'desire.' 5. ud- 'wet.'

B. From the following noun stems make the locative singular by adding the suffix -i.

1. vana- 'forest.' 2. antarikṣa- 'sky.'

C. From the following noun stems make the dative singular by adding the suffix -e and then the suffix -a.

1. deva- 'god.' 2. nala- 'Nala.'

D. From the following noun stems make the dative singular by adding the suffix -e, with guṇa of the final stem-vowels i and u.

1. agni- 'fire.' 2. śatru- 'enemy.' 3. pitṛ- 'father.'

E. From the following noun stems make the instrumental singular by adding the suffix -ā.

1. bhū- 'earth.' 2. strī- 'woman.' 3. sakhi- 'friend.'
4. nārī- 'woman.' 5. juhū- 'ladle.' 6. mātṛ- 'mother.'
7. nāu- 'ship.' 8. go- 'bull, cow.'

Exercise 6

A. Add the locative plural suffix -su to the following noun stems; change final a of the stem to e, except in numerals. In numbers 5, 6, and 12 external sandhi rules do not apply.

1. agni- 'fire.' 2. ṛtu- 'season.' 3. kusuma- 'flower.'
4. kriyā- 'action.' 5. gṝ- 'song.' 6. catur- 'four (men).'
7. tārā- 'star.' 8. dik- 'direction.' 9. dviṭ- 'enemy.'
10. pañca- 'five.' 11. pitṛ- 'father.' 12. pṝ- 'city.'
13. marut- 'wind.' 14. ratna- 'jewel.' 15. rājñī- 'queen.'

B. Add the 2d singular active suffix -si to the following stems.

1. bhava- 'become.' 2. yunak- 'join, yoke.' 3. ruṇat- 'obstruct.'

With guṇa of the root vowel (where possible).

4. i- 'go.' 5. han- 'slay.'

With guṇa of the second vowel (where possible).

6. juhu- 'sacrifice.' 7. dadā- 'give.' 8. bibhī- 'fear.'
9. bibhṛ- 'bear.' 10. sunu- 'press out.'

Exercise 7

Add to the following noun stems the genitive plural suffix, which is -ām after consonants and -n-ām after vowels; if the final phoneme of the stem is a short vowel, it is lengthened in this form.

1. agni- 'fire.' 2. ṛtu- 'season.' 3. kusuma- 'flower.'
4. kriyā- 'action.' 5. grāma- 'village.' 6. ghoṣa- 'noise.'
7. tārā- 'star.' 8. nakṣatra- 'constellation.' 9. nagarī- 'town.'
10. pakṣin- 'bird.' 11. pitṛ- 'father.' 12. brahman- 'priest; prayer.' 13. rajaka- 'washerman.' 14. ratna- 'jewel.'
15. raśmi- 'cord.' 16. rājñī- 'queen.' 17. varṇa- 'color.'
18. śastra- 'weapon.' 19. senā- 'army.' 20. vartman- 'path.'

Exercise 8

Make 2d singular and 3d singular present indicative forms from the following roots by addition of guṇated -nu- and after it -si and -ti respectively.

1. aś- 'attain.' 2. āp- 'obtain.' 3. ṛdh- 'thrive.'
4. kṣi- 'destroy.' 5. ci- 'gather.' 6. tṛp- 'be pleased.' (Note W710.) 7. du- 'be burned.' 8. dhṛṣ- 'dare.'
9. rādh- 'succeed.' 10. vṛ- 'cover.'

Exercise 9

A. From the following verb roots make the perfect passive participle by adding -ta-.

1. kṛṣ- 'pull, plow.' 2. iṣ- 'desire.' 3. krudh- 'be angry.'
4. stubh- 'praise.'

B. From the following verb roots make the 3d singular aorist with prefix a- and suffix -at.

1. chid- 'cut off.' 2. chṛd- 'vomit.'

C. From the following verb roots make the 3d plural present with infix -n- before the last consonant of the root, and addition of the suffix -anti or, when the root is preceded by *, the suffix -ate.

1. aj- 'anoint.' 2. *idh- 'kindle.' 3. ubh- 'cover over.'
4. chid- 'cut off.' 5. piṣ- 'crush.' 6. vic- 'sift.'
7. vṛj- 'twist.' 8. his- 'injure' (s exceptionally remains unaltered).

D. From the following verb roots make the 2d singular present with suffix -si and vṛddhi of a final root vowel u and guṇa of other root vowels.

1. ad- 'eat.' 2. nu- 'praise.' 3. han- 'kill.' 4. kṣi- 'rule.'
5. pṛ- 'pass.' 6. yam- 'reach.'

Exercise 10

Make the 2d and 3d singular present indicative from the following verb roots by addition of -si and -ti respectively, or, when preceded by an asterisk, -se and -te respectively.

1. *īś- 'be master.' 2. vac- 'speak.' 3. vaś- 'desire.'
4. *śiñj- 'twang.' 5. ad- 'eat.'

With guṇa of the root vowel.

6. dih- 'smear.' 7. *śī- 'lie down.'

With guṇa of the root vowel and insertion of -ī- between root and endings.

8. brū- 'say, speak.'

With vṛddhi of the root vowel.

9. sū- 'impel.' 10. stu- 'praise.'

Exercise 11

Make the 2d and 3d singular present indicative from the following verb roots by insertion of -na- before the last consonant of the root and addition of -si and -ti respectively, or, when preceded by an asterisk, by insertion of -n- and addition of -se and -te respectively.

1. aj- 'anoint.' 2. *idh- 'kindle.' 3. chid- 'cut off.'
4. piṣ- 'crush.' 5. bhaj- 'break.' 6. bhid- 'split.'
7. *bhuj- 'enjoy.' 8. yuj- 'join.' 9. rudh- 'obstruct.'
10. vic- 'sift.' 11. vṛj- 'twist.' 12. his-[1] 'injure' (in the 2d singular the rule -ss- > -ts- does not operate).

Exercise 12

From the following verb roots form the 3d singular present indicative by guṇa of the root vowel and adding the suffix -a- and then the suffix -ti, or -te when the root is preceded by an asterisk.

1. aj- 'drive.' 2. uṣ- 'burn.' 3. ṛc- 'praise.' 4. kṛṣ- 'plow.'
5. *kḷp- 'be suitable to.' 6. kruś- 'cry out.' 7. khan- 'dig.'
8. car- 'move.' 9. ji- 'conquer.' 10. tṝ- 'cross.'
11. dru- 'run.' 12. nī- 'lead.' 13. *pū- 'cleanse.'
14. *plu- 'float.' 15. *budh- 'be awakened.' 16. bhū- 'become.'
17. bhṛ- 'carry.' 18. yaj- 'sacrifice.' 19. *smi- 'smile.'
20. smṛ- 'remember.'

Exercise 13

From the following verb roots make the 3d singular future:

A. With the suffix -sya- and the suffix -ti (or -te when the root is preceded by an asterisk).

1. āp- 'obtain.' 2. kram- 'stride.' 3. jñā- 'know.'
4. tap- 'be hot, practice austerity.' 5. tyaj- 'abandon.'
6. dah- 'burn.' 7. dā- 'give.' 8. pac- 'cook.'

---

[1] This root is given by the grammarians as hiṃs-, but for the purpose of this exercise his- is more convenient.

9. pad- 'go, fall.' 10. prach- 'ask.' 11. *man- 'think.'
12. *ram- 'be pleased.' 13. *labh- 'take.' 14. vac- 'speak.'
15. vas- 'dwell.' 16. vah- 'carry.'

B. With the same suffixes and guṇa of the root vowel.

1. gup- 'protect.' 2. ci- 'gather.' 3. chid- 'cut off.'
4. ji- 'conquer.' 5. diś- 'point.' 6. nud- 'push.'
7. *budh- 'be awakened.' 8. bhid- 'split.' 9. *bhuj- 'enjoy.'
10. muc- 'release.' 11. yudh- 'fight.' 12. ruh- 'climb.'
13. viś- 'enter.' 14. *vṛt- 'turn.' 15. *śī- 'lie down.'
16. śru- 'hear.'

C. With the same suffixes and infixation of -n- before the last consonant of the root.

1. naś- 'be destroyed.'

Exercise 14

From the following verb roots make the perfect passive participle with the suffix -ta-; drop the nasal from those roots that have it before the final consonant.

1. añj- 'anoint.' 2. āp- 'obtain.' 3. i- 'go.' 4. idh- 'kindle.'
5. iṣ- 'desire.' 6. ūh- 'remove.' 7. kṛ- 'make.' 8. kṛt- 'cut.'
9. kruś- 'cry out.' 10. kṣubh- 'shake.' 11. guh- 'hide.'
12. cyu- 'move.' 13. ji- 'conquer.' 14. jñā- 'know.'
15. takṣ- 'fashion.' 16. tyaj- 'abandon.' 17. tras-'be terrified.'
18. dah- 'burn.' 19. naś- 'be lost.' 20. nah- 'tie.'
21. nī- 'lead.' 22. nud- 'push.' 23. pṛc- 'mix.'
24. bandh- 'bind.' 25. bhū- 'become' 26. bhraṃś- 'fall.'
27. mad- 'be intoxicated.' 28. muc- 'release.'
29, 30 (two forms). muh- 'be bewildered.' 31. mṛ- 'die.'
32. ruh- 'climb.' 33. limp- 'smear.' 34. vṛh- 'tear.'
35. śaṃs- 'praise.' 36. sah- 'overcome.'

Exercise 15

From the following verb roots make the perfect passive participle with the suffix -na-; drop the nasal from those roots that have it before the final consonant. The morphological statement dn > nn is applied; after this, internal sandhi rules operate. In 1, 12, 13, sandhi rules 59 and 60 apply, in spite of the heading before rule 59.

1. añc- 'bend.' 2. kṝ- 'scatter.' 3. kṣī- 'destroy.'
4. kṣud- 'crush.' 5. khid- 'tear.' 6. glā- 'be weary.'

7. chad- 'cover.' 8. tud- 'push.' 9. tṝ- 'cross.'
10. pad- 'go, fall.' 11. pṝ- 'fill.' 12. bhañj- 'break.'
13. ruj- 'break.' 14. sad- 'sit.' 15. skand- 'leap.'

Statements on reduplication and morphology in exercises 16-18 and 21-23

In exercises 16-18, the forms have an initial reduplication consisting of a consonant followed by a vowel. The vowel is a when the root vowel is ā̆ or ṛ, i when the root vowel is ī̆, u when the root vowel is ū̆. For the vowels in exercises 21-23, see the introductions to those exercises.

The consonant of the reduplication is the first consonant of the root, except that when an initial two-consonant cluster in the root consists of a stop preceded by a sibilant, the second consonant (i.e. the stop) is the one that is reduplicated.

If the consonant to be reduplicated is an aspirated stop, the consonant of the reduplication is the corresponding non-aspirated stop (e.g. bh⤳b).

If the consonant to be reduplicated is a velar or h, the consonant of the reduplication is the corresponding palatal (k⤳c, g⤳j), with non-aspiration also according to the previous statement (kh⤳c, gh⤳j, h⤳j).

In exercises 16 and 17, in the 3d singular active the root syllable shows: (1) vṛddhi if it has a final vowel or ă followed by a single consonant (ch is not a single consonant); (2) guṇa if the vowel is i, u, or ṛ followed by a consonant; (3) otherwise no change. In these two exercises, all other forms than the 3d singular active in general show the root syllable with vowel unchanged (except for the general sandhi changes, e.g. final ū̆ > uv before a vowel according to rule 38). But, the 3d plural in exercise 16, numbers 10, 13, and 16, loses the vowel a of the root syllable, and in exercise 16, numbers 14, 21, 25, 27, and 30, has no reduplication and replaces a by e.

Exercise 16

From the following verb roots form the 3d singular and 3d plural perfect indicative active with the endings -a and -us respectively, or, if an asterisk precedes the root, the middle with the endings -e and -ire respectively.

1. *kam- 'love.' 2. kāṅkṣ- 'desire.' 3. *kāś- 'appear.'
4. kup- 'be angry.' 5. kṛ- 'do, make.' 6. kram- 'stride.'
7. krudh- 'be angry.' 8. kliś- 'distress.' 9. kṣip- 'throw.'
10. khan- 'dig.' 11. gad- 'say.' 12. gup- 'protect.'

13. ghas- 'eat.' 14. car- 'move.' 15. chid- 'cut off.'
16. jan- 'bear (child).' 17. juṣ- 'enjoy.' 18. tud- 'push.'
19. tyaj- 'abandon.' 20. tras- 'be terrified.' 21. dah- 'burn.'
22. diś- 'point.' 23. dṛś- 'see.' 24. dhū- 'shake.'
25. pad- 'go, fall.' 26. prach- 'ask.' 27. phal- 'burst.'
28. bandh- 'bind.' 29. *budh- 'be awakened.' 30. bhaj- 'divide.'
31. bhī- 'fear.' 32. bhṛ- 'carry.' 33. bhram- 'wander.'

Exercise 17

From the following verb roots form the 3d singular and 3d plural perfect indicative active with the endings -a and -us respectively, or, if an asterisk precedes the root, middle with the endings -e and -ire respectively. In numbers 1 and 6 s does not become ṣ.

1. sku- 'tear.' 2. skhal- 'stumble.' 3. stu- 'praise.'
4. stṛ- 'scatter' (guṇa of root vowel in 3d plural).
5. *spṛdh- 'contend.' 6. sphuṭ- 'burst.' 7. smṛ- 'remember' (guṇa of root vowel in 3d plural). 8. sru- 'flow.'
9. svap- 'sleep' (this root should be treated as sup- for the vowel of the reduplication and for the 3d plural; the 3d singular has reverse vṛddhi).
10. ścut- 'drip.' 11. śru- 'hear.' 12 śliṣ- 'clasp.'

Exercise 18

From the following verb roots ending in ā form the 3d singular and 3d plural perfect indicative active, with -āu representing ā of the root plus -a of the ending in 3d singular, and with ā of the root lost before ending -us in the 3d plural.

1. khyā- 'tell.' 2. gā- 'sing.' 3. ghrā- 'smell.' 4. jñā- 'know.'
5. dhā- 'place.' 6. dhmā- 'blow.' 7. pā- 'drink.'
8. bhā- 'shine.' 9. mlā- 'wither.' 10. yā- 'go.'
11. sthā- 'stand.' 12. snā- 'bathe.' 13. hā- 'abandon.'

Exercise 19

Make two gerunds from each of the following verb roots, using the suffixes -tvā and -ya. After a root ending in a short vowel, add -t- before -ya. The roots ending in ā, except jñā, replace ā by i before -tvā. The two roots ending in a nasal plus another consonant lose the nasal in these forms. The four roots ending in a nasal lose the nasal before -tvā. Roots 10, 15, 19, and 20 are given with reverse guṇa; the gerunds have the basic vowels.

1. i- 'go.' 2. kṛ- 'do, make.' 3. gam- 'go.' 4. jñā- 'know.'
5. tṝ- 'cross.' 6. dah- 'burn.' 7. dṛś- 'see.'
8. dhā- 'place' (dh > h in the form with -tvā).
9. piṣ- 'crush.' 10. prach- 'ask.' 11. bandh- 'bind.'
12. budh- 'be awakened.' 13. man- 'think.' 14. mā- 'measure.'
15. yaj- 'sacrifice.' 16. yuj- 'join.' 17. ram- 'take pleasure.'
18. labh- 'receive.' 19. vac- 'speak.' 20. vas- 'dwell.'
21. śaṃs- 'praise.' 22. sic- 'pour out.' 23. sṛj- 'send forth, create.' 24. sthā- 'stand.' 25. han- 'strike, kill.'

Exercise 20

From the following verb roots make the gerundive with -ya-. The meaning is: from transitive roots 'which must be/is to be/will be ...,' from intransitive roots 'which must/is to/ will ....'

A.

1. vad- 'say.' 2. guh- 'conceal.'

B. ā is replaced by e.

3. dā- 'give.' 4. dhā- 'place.'

C. Guṇa, and -t- before -ya-.

5. mṛ- 'die.'

D and E. Final guṇa and vṛddhi diphthongs are treated before -ya- as they are before vowels.

D. Guṇa.

6. dviṣ- 'hate.' 7. śī- 'lie down' (make the feminine of the gerundive with ā replacing a of the suffix: 'bed').
8. hu- 'pour.'

E. Vṛddhi.

9. kṛ- 'do, make.' 10. bhū- 'become.' 11. vac- 'say.'
12. vṛ- 'ward off.'

Exercise 21

From the following verb roots make two forms each for the 3d singular present indicative of the intensive. The forms have reduplication; the reduplicating vowel is guṇa when the vowel of the root is ĭ or ŭ, and ā when the vowel of the root is a. The consonant of the reduplication is to be determined from the section preceding exercise 16.

The first form is active and is like the root class or the reduplicating class of the present, i.e. with guṇa of the root vowel and the 3d singular ending -ti.

The second form is middle, with -ya- between the root and the 3d singular ending -te.

1. bhū- 'become, be' (meaning: 'be in the habit of').
2. lih- 'lick' (meaning: 'lick greedily').
3. lup- 'bewilder' (meaning: 'bewilder exceedingly').
4. yaj- 'sacrifice' (meaning: 'sacrifice often').
5. hrī- 'be ashamed' (meaning: 'be greatly ashamed').

Exercise 22

Desiderative forms. Make the 3d singular active with -a-ti; but, when * precedes the root, make the 3d singular middle with -a-te, and when ** precedes the root, make the adjective with -u.

The forms have reduplication; the reduplicating vowel is i when the vowel of the root is ā̆, ṛ, or i, and u when the vowel of the root is u. In all the forms except numbers 2 and 3 the vowel of the root syllable remains unchanged; in numbers 2 and 3 the vowel of the root syllable is lost entirely. After the root syllable the desiderative suffix -s- is added.

1. dah- 'burn' (meaning: 'is about to burn'). 2. dā- 'give.'
3. dhā- 'place' (apply rule 54). 4. **nud- 'push.'
5. budh- 'be awakened, know' (meaning: 'desires to know').
6. *bhuj- 'enjoy.' 7. muc- 'release.' 8. vas- 'dwell' (see rule 72). 9. vid- 'know, find.' 10. viś- 'enter.'
11. sthā- 'stand.' 12. **spṛś- 'touch' (rule 46 does not work after i, because of the following ṣ).

Exercise 23

Aorist of the causative. Make the 3d singular with the prefix a- and the ending -a-t. The forms have reduplication; the reduplicating vowel is short or long i when the vowel of the root is a, ī̆, or ṛ, and short or long u when the vowel of the root is u. The quantity of the vowel in the reduplicating syllable is either V[CCV or V̄[CV; the former is found when the vowel of the following syllable (being followed by a single consonant) is long, the latter when it is short.

1. grah- 'seize.' 2. chid- 'split.' 3. dīp- 'shine.'
4. dṛś- 'see.' 5. dru- 'run.' 6. nam- 'bow.'
7. mīl- 'close the eyes.' 8. yuj- 'join.' 9. śri- 'rest on.'

With guṇa in root syllable.

10. kṛ- 'make.' 11. bhṛ- 'carry.' 12. śī- 'lie down.'

Exercise 24

From the following verb roots form primary noun derivatives with the suffixes indicated. Where possible, the root vowels show guṇa in the derivatives.

Suffix -a-:

1. diś- 'point' (meaning: 'spot, region').
2. du- 'burn' (meaning: 'forest fire').
3. duṣ- 'spoil' (meaning: 'fault').
4. duh- 'milk' (meaning: 'milking, milk')
5. bhṛ- 'carry' (meaning: 'carrying, weight').

Suffix -ana-:

6. i- 'go' (meaning: 'path')
7. dṛś- 'see' (meaning: 'sight').
8. bhāṣ- 'speak' (meaning: 'speech').
9. math- 'stir, churn' (meaning: 'churning').
10. mṛ- 'die' (meaning: 'death').
11. ru- 'roar' (meaning: 'roar').
12. sthā- 'stand' (meaning: 'position').

Suffix -tṛ- 'one who does':

13. kṛ- 'make.' 14. ji- 'conquer.' 15. dṛś- 'see' (with reverse guṇa). 16. bhuj- 'enjoy.' 17. yaj- 'sacrifice.'
18. yuj- 'join, yoke.' 19. vac- 'speak.' 20. vid- 'know.'

Exercise 25

From the following verb roots form primary noun derivatives with the suffix -ti-. Roots 5 and 8 are given by the grammarians with reverse guṇa, and the derivatives show the basic vowels.

1. diś- 'point out, grant' (meaning: 'good fortune').
2. pṝ- 'fill' (meaning: 'completion, bestowal').
3. bhaj- 'divide, adore' (meaning: 'division, devotion').
4. muc- 'release' (meaning: 'release').

5. yaj- 'sacrifice' (meaning: 'sacrifice').
6. yuj- 'join' (meaning: 'union').
7. ruh- 'ascend, increase' (meaning: 'ascent, increase, conventional meaning of a word').
8. vac- 'speak' (meaning: 'speech').
9. vid- 'find' (meaning: 'acquisition').
10. vṛdh- 'increase' (meaning: 'increase').
11. sū- 'beget, bear' (meaning: 'birth').
12. sṛj- 'emit, create' (meaning: 'creation')
13. smṛ- 'remember' (meaning: 'memory, tradition').

Exercise 26

From the following noun stems form secondary noun and adjective derivatives by addition of the indicated suffixes. The secondary derivatives have vṛddhi of the first syllable of the underlying word and guṇa of the last syllable of the underlying word.

Suffix -a-:

1. indu- 'moon' (meaning: 'lunar').
2. ṛtu- 'season' (meaning: 'seasonable').
3. suṣṭhu 'excellently' (meaning: 'excellence'; the underlying form is not a noun, but an adverb).

Suffix -ya-:

4. araṇi- 'firestick' (meaning: 'pertaining to the firesticks').
5. indumatī- 'Indumatī (a woman)' (meaning: 'descendant of Indumatī').
6. ṛṣi- 'a sage' (meaning: 'descendant of a sage').
7. eṇī- 'female antelope' (meaning: 'produced from female antelope').
8. kuntī- 'Kuntī (a woman)' (meaning: 'son of Kuntī').
9. jamadagni- 'Jamadagni (a man)' (meaning: 'son of Jamadagni').
10. bhaginī- 'sister' (meaning: 'sister's son').

Exercise 27

From the following root nouns (namely, 1 and 2) and noun stems form the basic forms of the nominative singular, instrumental plural, and locative plural, with suffixes zero, -bhis, and -su respectively; note that before the latter two suffixes the rules of external sandhi apply, but not in 1 and 2 before -su. When two stem forms are given, the first is that of the nominative singular, the second that of the instrumental and locative plural.

1. gṝ- 'song.' 2. pṝ- 'city.' 3. āśīs- 'blessing.'
4. dos- 'forearm.' 5. ahar-/ahas- 'day.' 6. dant/dat- 'tooth.'
7. sraj- 'wreath.' 8. asṛj-/asa- 'blood.' 9. vaṇij- 'merchant.'
10. tvac- 'skin.' 11. upānah- 'shoe' (the verb root nah- is involved, with its special treatment of h).

www.ingramcontent.com/pod-product-compliance
Lightning Source LLC
Chambersburg PA
CBHW021717230426
43668CB00008B/862
* 9 7 8 0 5 2 0 3 3 2 8 0 5 *